A Morgan, la primavera.

A dicembre, un pettirosso

La fine dell'inverno

La primavera
è arrivata
di nuovo
e le margherite
stanno sbocciando
come
il nostro amore

Non le colgo
non le lascio
seccare
fra le pagine
del libro
che mi hai donato
in attesa
dell'inverno

Il vento
mi ricorda
che il gelo
è sempre pronto
ad insinuarsi
nelle mie fragili ossa

e tu
potresti migrare
verso terre
più calde,
più stabili

Ma sei
il mio girasole
e la mia luce,
e mi prenderò cura
di te
stagione dopo stagione,
mentre
le margherite
sfioriscono
e tu cresci,
splendido
e luminoso,
e sarò
la tua terra
se vorrai
mettere radici

(Post) Love Letter

Promises are
meant to be
broken
I know that,
I know
but I gave you
a promise ring
anyway
and now
it sits in
the pink box,
waiting to be
forgotten

I'm trying
to forget
the spark
in your blue eyes
the warmth
of your arms
the words
you said and meant
But they never
quite matched

your actions

And I'm not
shitting on
what we once
called us
It was good
it was tender
it was perfect
it was precious
it was great,
even when
it wasn't
when I wasn't
when you,
yes you
you weren't

Now I let
our songs
fade into
background noise
the poetry
is still there
but the spark

is gone
Because you
let me down
your selfishness
poisoned my heart
and stained
our memories,
painted them
with a darker
colour

But the sun
shines
on my beloved
snowy mountains
and the anger
won't last forever
and I'm writing you
a post-love letter
because
time eases
the ache,
but
I can't forget you

I still love you

March (in the rain)

You left me
alone
in the rain
for five long months
and when
I found
the sun again
you cried
that your flowers
are dying

Who will
take care
of my soil,
now?

I cannot be
your blue sky
your sun
your rain
the gentle wind
that guides
your petals,

not anymore

Not after
you gave me
just enough
warmth
for my drenched
land
not to drown
and
took my thorns
one by one
until my skin
was bare
and tender

Do you like
the taste
of blood?
The same
taste that
keeps me
awake at
night,

while I watch
the stars die
and the moon
hides and
weeps
for her child

Bleed, kid
you know
that first love
never lasts

Father, I am a rich man / heart made of gold

You judge
my lovers
by their bank account
by the colours
that flow
in their veins
You don't even
know half of them

Her, she was
a different kind
of first love
I was
a kid
but the butterflies
were the same

And her,
the definition
of right person,
wrong time

Do you remember

that big, red package?
From them, "just
a friend"
Broke my heart,
but the pain
was sublime

Him, you actually
know him
never thought badly
of him,
because all you saw
was his wealth
All I saw
was someone
who didn't even
exist
I created him

You will never know
what he did
to me

Is this
what you hope for?
For me
to marry a wealthy man

Father,
I am a rich man
but you refuse
to see
the man
and the richness inside
those emotions
that make you scoff
but they're
the most precious thing
I own

This heart
is made
of gold

Replay

Quante volte
hai parlato
alla luna
chiedendole
di scacciare
l'oscurità?

Quante volte
hai pregato
il sole
di non sorgere
per non
ricordare
che non c'è
speranza?

Stella cadente,
i tuoi luminosi
frammenti
accendono
il mio cuore
di dolore
e amore

E la nostalgia
è un cielo
senza nuvole
ma senza
luce

Dammi le ali

Inconcepibile, per te
la felicità
di un altro colore
di un'altra forma

Inconcepibile, per te
la libertà
in un tumulto
di colori
di fiori

Dove tu
vedi un
rimpianto sicuro,
io vedo
creazione
La tua
distruzione,
per me
un inno divino
e dannatamente
umano

all'autenticità
più pura

Padre,
dammi le ali
quelle cicatrici
sul petto
prima che
si dipingano
sui miei polsi

Modern Love Letter

Can I have
the last apple?
Yes,
yes you can
it was
waiting for you

I open
the window
so you can
smoke
and while
you do,
I take
the coke
out of
the fridge

Can I borrow-
... my sweatpants?
... my t-shirt?
... my oxygen?
My darling,
you can

keep it
if it means
you exist
for one more
second

I wander
in every shop
and I
look for
a piece
of you
a plushie,
or
something spiky,
maybe
or
pencils
and markers
and highlighters

Can I stay
the night?
Oh love,

please stay
for the rest
of my life
(But if
you have
to leave
I hope
the wind
kisses your cheeks
and
the sun
never sleeps
so each step
you take
will be
in the light)

I play
Queen,
Mother Mother,
and even
that song
you despise,
just to
make you laugh

make you sing
make you dance
with me, clumsily

My robin,
so small
and soft
and fierce
blooming red,
your heart
You painted
the winter away
from my soul

Self-sabotage

We dress up
as villains
we play
our roles
for our own
entertainment
but when
we take off
the masks
your face is
angelic and pure
and I am
the bad guy

I'm holding
the dagger
so tight
blood drips
from my fingers

Run,
before I
lose control

It's okay
if I am
the one bleeding
but you have
to run
before I
start chasing
you

Run,
please
I can't tame
the monster

(You deserve better
This was
too good
for my wretched
soul, anyway)

I want you
to stay
but really,
you should

run away

(You can't
tame me)

I am you / you are me

Don't run
from me
Don't try
to fight me
You need me
You know
you need me

Let me in
I'll be gentle
Feed me
let me feast
on the shadows
your mind casts

Don't be scared
you know me,
don't you?
We are friends

I am you

And you are
me

You can
let the light in
but when you
look in the mirror
you know
you can't drown
me out

Poor little thing,
you're a crumpled up
piece of paper
now, lying
on the bathroom
floor
and I am
the hand
that crushed
you

Dream of me, I'll dream of you

You say
our paths
will cross again
but I
don't believe
in falling stars
and red strings
anymore

And you used
to say
dream of me
so I did
but even
in my dreams
you didn't
love me
the same
anymore

Do you ever
dream of me,
too?
And if you do,

do you embrace me
and kiss my forehead?
Do you smile
and laugh with me?
Or do you watch my
back
as you grab my hips?

When I
close my eyes
I see your face
and I
want to cry
but when
you close
your eyes
you only see
the night

Family / inner child

Father,
tell me
this gift
of yours
where can I
put it
when I don't
need it
anymore
when I don't
want it
anymore?

Your anger
has kept me
alive
for enough time,
now
I think my fire
has been fed
enough
and it can
survive
on its own

Mother,
tell me
this void
you left me
will it always
be painful
to look at
to touch?

Your absence
has taught me
to love everyone
but myself
and yet
the seed
I planted
is timidly growing

Sister,
tell me
what is it like
to have a brother
are you

ashamed
of me?

If you are
you hide it
so well,
now

Come, child
we're safe
I've got
hugs for you
and tissues
to wipe
your tears
and ears
to listen
to your pain

Baby,
I'm sorry
I'm so sorry
you don't have
to forgive them
but forgive
yourself
forgive me
for the mistakes
I still make

And one day,
I hope
you'll be
proud of me
just like I am
proud of you

March (in the sun)

The shadows
of the trees
painted on
the streets
make me
tear up

They're alive

The sun
kisses
the flowers
and they
smile at it
it kisses
my face
my hands
my heart

I'm alive

Warm
and loud
is my friends'
laughter
on the stairs,
in between
the courses
Warm
and pink
is the sunset
when my
shoulders
relax
against the wall
Warm
and sparkly
are your emerald green
eyes
while you lay
next to me
in the dry,
luscious grass
of March,
in the sun

You're alive

It's March
and my soul
muses about
the sunny days

Non ho mai capito nulla di fisica

Ho fatto un sogno.

Il cielo
era blu,
blu notte
estate,
forse
e tu eri
con lei
non le sei
mai piaciuto
ma a me sì,
a me tanto

Mi ha detto
che siete amici,
adesso
e io
non ho osato
avvicinarmi
chissà
se mi avresti
riconosciuto
cosa avresti fatto?

cosa avresti detto?

Forse
prendiamoci un caffè
quello che
mi offristi
tre anni fa

Forse
scusa
per non aver
mai risposto
alla tua lettera

Forse
ti penso
anch'io,
a volte

Chissà
come mi immagini
come la creatura
spaventata e
fragile

che ero
o magari
come il lupo
solitario
che ho
smesso di
essere

Ma che
importanza ha?

Era un sogno.

Melody

Nuove ossessioni
prendono il posto
di vecchie passioni
e il mio cuore
non è mai sazio

Ho amore
da dare
a ogni libro
ancora da
stampare
a ogni canzone
ancora da
registrare

E crescere
è una scoperta
che non fa più
così paura

Ma a volte
l'orizzonte
è troppo ampio
e l'anima
cerca rifugio

in ogni nicchia

Il calore di cinque
mai provato
sulla pelle
è casa,
il mio
cielo di stelle

Così torno
nel conforto
dei miei ricordi
la musica è
la mia guida
la mia ancora
di salvezza

E nell'abbraccio
di mille voci
la mia anima
riposa

Mordimi

Non mi fai bene
sei veleno
nelle mie vene

La mente
non riesce
a fare pace
col cuore

Era giusto
lasciarti andare
era necessario
ma ogni secondo
che ci allontana
da noi
e il presente
è sul mio petto
un macigno
opprimente

Vorrei implorarti
di tornare
ma non possiamo
più permetterci
di sbagliare

Fine,
fine,
fine

(Ma a una parte
di me
non dispiacerebbe
morire
fra le tue
spire)

Soulmate

You say
we're meant to be
we're destined
I refuse
to believe that
but maybe
maybe we are

You're not
as great
as I painted you
to be
and I am
just a little
too fucked up
to deserve
any better

So come,

fate
take out
your red string
tie me
to him
tie him
to me
no need
to make it
tight
I cannot
run away
from my feelings,
anyway

He's in my
head,
I must confess

Mud

\- Morning -

It's a rainy day
without the rain
the sky is grey
and the air tastes
like a soft sadness
a sweet melancholy

It's bittersweet
the wet dirt
on the tip
of my tongue

\- Evening –

Come, rain
wash away
this feeling
wash me away
fill the grey hole
inside my chest
I want
to cry
until I am
clean

April / fool

I want to be
the boy
that brings you
flowers
and apples
and plushies

I want to be
the boy
that makes you
laugh
every single day

I want to be
the snowflakes
that dance around
your pretty face

on this cold April day

But I am
a sad mess
I am just
a kid
even though
I've seen the moon
rise a few more times
than you have
and my heart
is fragile
but, perhaps
I am enough
to make you
smile

If you must ask me how much I love you

You're made of
little,
sweet,
pretty
things

Every scar
on your body
is filled
with gold
and flowers

And I'm made of
music,
words
and love

Don't ever
doubt
that I
adore you

But if you must

ask me
how much I
love you,
well

If every star
was my love
for you,
the sky
would be
bright
all night

If every snowflake,
too,
was my love
for you,
then
the Earth
would be
covered
in snow
every day,

every season

And
I can't live
forever
neither can
you
but my words,
I hope,
will make you
immortal

That is
all I ask

of them
that is
all I want
for you
to exist
in them
even when
we're both
gone

That is
how much
I love you

Un messaggio di speranza

Non hai bisogno
di diventare
nulla che tu
non sia già
perché tu
sei il sole
quello di marzo
apparso dopo
un lungo inverno
e fai sbocciare
i fiori
fai sbocciare
sorrisi

A dicembre,
un pettirosso
una mattina
mi diede il buongiorno
minuscolo e
spavaldo
fronteggiò
la morte
sulla mia spalla
il suo fiato
gelido
nelle mie ossa

Portava un
messaggio
di speranza:
il tuo arrivo

Your hoodie

I used to live
in your hoodie
your favourite
hoodie
just to feel
the comfort of
your arms
the safety of
your hands
the warmth of
your heart

I've been cold
for a month
now
I live
in someone else's
hoodie
but its warmth
can't fill
the hole
in my chest
that you left

I had to
leave
actually
we both
know that

I just
didn't think
you'd haunt me
like this
a ghost hug,
some days
a bittersweet rain,
faint like
the kisses
I taste on
my lips
when I wake up

I will spend
forever
missing something
impossible

08.04

In the darkest hours
the moon shines
the brightest
just like
in my darkest days
you bring me
comfort and solace

I want
to live
for you
but
I also want
to live
with you

And I
don't know
what to do
with my hands

Follow the clouds

You say
we can be friends
when you can
bear to
talk to me
again

Don't you realize
that in a month
or five
in a year
or more
we're still
going to be
two strangers
with two years
of memories?

Don't you understand
that I cannot
forgive you,

not anymore?

I can't fix
what you broke
I can't go
back to
those times
and stop myself
from loving you
over all the hurt
that you inflicted
that I hid so well

The clouds were right
I should've followed
them,
should've followed
their advice

It was enough

loml

I should know
by now
that I can't have
everything
I want

I can't
have you
and be myself

I can't
sing
"How I miss you so,
light of my life"
to them
and expect you

to sing it back
to me

But, sometimes
I miss you
more than
I should
and I
dream that
you stay
a little longer
in the endless
moonlit night
and we don't
need another life
to get it right

Questions (voices)

Where did
the happy days
go?
Where did
the January luck
run to?
I stared
at the mirror
for so long
trying to catch
my smile,
make it stay
a little longer
How could it
escape?

How can
my world
come crashing
down on
my shoulders
again?
Why so soon?

It's like
three years ago
I'm wandering
in the dark
and I keep
falling
falling
falling
and you're
not there

Why do you
say you
love me
as if
it is
the answer
to all my questions?
Why is it
not enough
to be the answer?
When did it
stop being enough?

How could I
let this happen
again?
I keep blaming
myself
for the voices
inside my head
they don't even
belong to me

A luci spente

Quattro giorni
per innamorarsi
un messaggio
per spezzarmi
il cuore

Il cielo
è sempre
più grigio
mentre stacco
le polaroid
dalle luci
ma non piove

Ho freddo
le mie mani
tremano
ad ogni
mio respiro

ma non mi
riscaldo
con la felpa
che mi hai
restituito
per paura
che il tuo profumo
svanisca

Ecco, è tutto
impacchettato
tutto finito
la pagina
è stata voltata
di nuovo
ma io sono
prigioniero
dell'inchiostro
ancora fresco

No more light (life)

I only like
my reflection
in the window
after midnight
like a modern
vampire that
craves the sunlight
and the delightful
burning pain
but is too much
of a coward
to die
like that
even though
I've been undead
for nine centuries

I wasn't done loving you

Tonight
I almost
text you
goodnight
but I don't
I can't

I wasn't done
loving you
I wish
I could
tell you
you're beautiful
I'm proud of you
I love you
one last time

Tonight
I don't get
to make you
smile
the stars
on my ceiling

are just plastic
I don't get
to kiss you
goodbye
I replay
your voice messages
but they
are just
empty words
that fill
happy memories

Last night
you closed
the door
but I have
nowhere to go
so I wait
on your doorstep
no winter
is cold enough
to stop
my burning love

XI

Sei come
le crepe
delle radici
sotto l'asfalto
più deglutisco
più la mia gola
è arida
e tu lì,
incastrato
fra cuore
e lacrime
che tentano
di fuggire

Come faccio
ad andare avanti
se ad ogni
tua sporgenza
inciampo
e le ferite

non si
chiudono,
mai
e io
con le unghie
le riapro
ancora,
ancora,
ancora

Ero
una persona
migliore
quando
c'eri tu

Ero
a casa
quando
c'eri tu

Eclipse

In the morning
I'm fine
but at night
I want
to die
and I almost
text you
how much
I miss you
and that
I used
to love
your height
but now
everything stands
in your shadow
and I am
withering
without
your warm love

No better days

The sink
is full
it doesn't
get
any better

This place
is a mess,
you say
have you
seen my mind
I ask

Bare walls
smiles that
faded
after
the pictures
were taken

That name
means
"God's home"
I still am

a home
to anyone
who needs
a safe place
a light
some warmth

A home
to anyone
but myself

I have
no warmth
for myself
I have
no light
for myself
so I
shiver
in the dark
I have
no better days
I live
in gray

No more time
to flow
let me
evaporate
and become
the rain
to kiss
your tears

Alzati, respira

La vita
deve andare avanti,
tesoro,
anche quando
il sole sorge
ma tu no,
tu resti
nell'abbraccio
confortante
delle coperte
anche quando
il lutto
per gli anni
che non riavrai
mai indietro
ti soffoca

Alzati,
respira

Le lacrime
scorrono inarrestabili,
sì
e l'ossigeno
s'incastra
nei singhiozzi
ma il tuo cuore
pompa
il tuo sangue
guizza

E tu
devi riprovarci
lo devi
ad ogni giorno
di pioggia
che hai affrontato
ad ogni notte
insonne
che hai superato

Girasoli

Tutto ciò
che le tue mani
incontrano
distruggono
non si fermano
neanche
alla tua stessa
essenza

Ma poi
i tuoi polpastrelli
toccano me
e rimettono insieme

i miei cocci
e con ogni
tuo sguardo
mi ridipingi
con le tue
labbra soffici
mi aggiusti

Con ogni
tuo respiro
fai di me
un'opera d'arte

RINGRAZIAMENTI

Ai miei lettori e alle mie lettrici vecchi e nuovi, silenziosi e non, la mia costante. Grazie del supporto, della pazienza, della comprensione, dell'affetto e dell'entusiasmo con cui accogliete ogni mia nuova storia e raccolta.

Grazie al pettirosso che, una mattina di dicembre 2021, si presentò sulle scale all'uscita del mio palazzo e mi diede la forza di non gettare la spugna.

Grazie a J, la mia luna.

Grazie ai miei più cari amici, che rendono la mia vita degna di essere vissuta e apprezzata tramite le mie parole.

www.ingramcontent.com/pod-product-compliance
Lightning Source LLC
Chambersburg PA
CBHW051403150726
48000CB00003B/1307